In the Garden

In the garden,
I found a caterpillar
crawling on a branch.

In the garden,
I found a dandelion
growing by a fence.

In the garden,
I found a lizard
hiding in the grass.

In the garden,
I found a snail
sliding along a log.

In the garden,
I found a creeper
climbing up the wall.

In the garden,
I found a dewdrop
sitting in a flower.

In the garden,
I found a spiderweb
hanging on a tree.

In the garden,
I found Grandpa
sleeping in the sun!